POLISH
your
KITCHEN
CHRISTMAS EDITION

A book of memories

by Anna Hurning

Printed in the United States of America

First printing, 2019

P.Y.K. Anna Hurning
orderpyk@gmail.com

Food Photography © by Anna Hurning
Portrait © by Malina Majewska @malinamajewska.com
Design by Igor Wypijewski @korektura.pl

polishyourkitchen.com

ISBN Paperback: 978-1-7342488-0-7
ISBN eBook: 978-1-7342488-1-4

For Hanna

CONTENTS

MEET ANNA

Ever since I came to the U.S. for the first time in 1993 as an exchange student, I have been asked for recipes for the food I cooked or dishes that friends knew from when they were kids that their grandma made. I landed in Wisconsin, an area saturated with 2nd, 3rd or even later generations of Polish and Eastern European immigrants. Conversations about food were always prominent.

Growing up, I was mostly influenced by my grandma (Babcia) Stasia's cooking. She spent a lot of time with us and was the primary cook in our home. I curiously watched and "recorded" everything she did in my head. We had a large kitchen with a huge island in the middle, enough room to spread pasta to dry, pierogi lined up for boiling, or rows and rows of jars waiting for pickles in preparation for the winter. Babcia let me "help", while patiently explaining the exact measurements of "a little bit". Cooking became art in her hands. No written recipe, no cookbooks, no professional training, and yet somehow it always came out exactly the same.

My dearest Babcia Stasia passed away at the age of 89 in 2016. With her guidance in my heart, I've been perfecting her recipes for years. I've recreated many and I've simplified and adjusted them to suit the ingredients that were available in the U.S. My cooking may not compare to Babcia's, but since I've craved flavors of home ever since I left Poland, I had to keep trying to get it right.

In 2018, after 23 years in the service, my husband retired from the Army and we decided to move our Polish-American family to Poland. It was the best decision for us. I love being close to my family again, my husband is appreciating the European way of living and our daughter can finally be spoiled by her grandparents year-round.

Recipes that you see here come from my family's table or are my renditions of new dishes I taste around the country. All photography is also done by me. I continue to learn from my mom and dad and explore Polish regional cooking while traveling through Poland.

I hope you find many inspirations here and some will even bring back memories of flavors from your Polish home.

Happy cooking and smacznego!

Anna Hurning

INTRODUCTION

My Dear Hungry Friends,

I'd like to invite you to experience a Polish Christmas with me this year. Please come in and see what this special holiday looks like at my family table. I'm warning you from the start though, you won't see any gołąbki or kiełbasa here. This is Polish Christmas: traditional cooking and strict rules apply.

I know some of you may say: "my family came from Poland and they DO, INDEED, cook gołąbki, and kiełbasa for Christmas", and this may be true. Consider this, however. As generations of Poles immigrated to the "new continent", the Polish kitchen evolved. Traditions changed due to availability of ingredients and environment. Immigrants adjusted and cooked dishes that reminded them of home, especially during "special occasions", like Christmas. Some dishes faded away from their menus altogether. Second, third and following generations were left with just a taste of what Polish cooking can be. I hope you keep an open mind and consider bringing some of those classic dishes back into your home, and keep the traditions alive.

Recipes that you see in this book are to this day prepared and served by the masses in Poland. Some dishes may vary, but there is a consensus on certain items. Beet soup with dumplings, pierogi with sauerkraut and mushrooms, fried fish, Greek-style fish, herring and a few others, are always present. The method of cooking may be different from home chef to home chef, but you can expect to see this or a similar menu all around the country.

Traditions

When I was growing up, I didn't really get the "holiday feeling" until Christmas Eve. This is when we got and decorated our tree, and this is when I could start smelling all those smells that remind me of Christmas: sauerkraut being at the top of that list. Up until recently, decorating the Christmas tree was done on Christmas Eve, or maybe a day before at the earliest. Now, you see tree stands all around the city at the beginning of December.

Poles will celebrate Christmas for three days, enough for the cheer to last us the next 12 months. The main meal is served on Christmas Eve, and then there are two more days when we continue with festivities: first and second Day of Christmas refers to 25th and 26th of December.

Wigilia (Christmas Eve dinner) was always the most important day of the holidays for my family, normally spent with closest relatives, traditionally eating meatless dishes only. Tradition of meatless Christmas Eve has changed a bit recently and the rules on eating meat that day were loosened in the Catholic Church. We now eat bigos, a sauerkraut dish with meat in it, and sometimes the beet or mushroom soup is made based on a meat stock. Many Poles strictly stick to the tradition though, and on Christmas Eve serve meatless dishes only.

Dinner starts when the first star shows up on the still pale blue sky. My brother and I were in charge of looking for it when we were kids. Good way to keep us out of the kitchen, I guess. We were extra hungry by then, as we could only get away with sneaking cold pierogi a couple of times that day.

Preparation

Preparation for Christmas Eve dinner at my house starts early, and I'm not talking about shopping for gifts. Everybody knows that cabbage has to sour for bigos and pierogi for at least 10 days. As soon as I start cooking sauerkraut, my husband says it smells like Christmas. And I agree.

Christmas, to me, also smells like oranges. During the communist time in Poland, Christmas was the only time we would get oranges (if we were lucky); not because we couldn't afford them, but because there weren't any available. We would get them in our gift bags under the tree, along with some sweets. My brother and I had to compare who got how many and how big, just to make sure it was even and fair.

Dinner table

Setting the dinner table was my job, and I was so proud of it. I was instructed to cover it with a white tablecloth and set the fancy china and silverware saved for special occasions. We also added one additional place setting for an unexpected guest. Tradition dictates that if someone knocked on your door that night, you should let the person in, and invite him or her to join you for dinner. You will see Poles follow this tradition still.

We also place a handful of hay under the tablecloth, to symbolize the manger.

Best wishes

For my family, Christmas Eve dinner starts with all family members sharing "opłatek" (a thin wafer, kind of like the one you get at communion) by everyone breaking a piece of the one you're holding, eating it, and wishing each other Merry Christmas and other appropriate wishes for the upcoming year.

Food

Then is the fun part... food!! Minimum of 12 dishes to represent the 12 Apostles (in some parts of Poland, 13) are present. These dishes vary just a bit from region to region, and home to home, but all include some of the favorites you will find in this book. Everyone will taste a bit of each dish, carefully judging how many more there are to try, just to make sure there is room for dessert.

When I prepare this elaborate Christmas Eve dinner, I try to plan so all the dishes are hot and served at once. I heat the soup ahead of time and store in a thermos (normally not enough room to keep multiple pots on the stove), I brown pierogi in a pan, transfer onto a serving dish and keep in the oven set to warm. Cabbage dishes are also heated up, also transferred onto oven safe serving dishes before joining the rest in the oven. I boil potatoes (for the herring in sour cream), drain them, let them steam for a few seconds, cover back up, wrap in a towel and stuff into my bed, to keep hot. This is a popular Polish method I'm sure you've seen done by your family before. It works great! Dried fruit juice will also be poured into glasses and served ahead of time.

Cold dishes are obviously stored in the fridge, plated, just ready to be placed on the table. The very last thing I prepare is the fried fish. Carp is pan sautéed and will go into the oven for just a minute. We are ready to eat now, but the breaking of the wafer comes first. As soon as we have fully blessed each other with best wishes of health and great fortune, we will be ready to eat!

When I was a young lady, my grandparents always wished me that I find a nice boy. These wishes, paired with a generous kiss were a path to guaranteed success, according to them. And yes, they were right. I did find a nice boy!

We normally start with a small serving of hot barszcz z uszkami (beetroot soup with mushroom-filled dumplings) and a small serving of mushroom soup. After that, everyone will grab what they like the most. I continue with fish dishes: cold herring in sour cream served over hot potatoes and fried carp. Those two (after pierogi and barszcz) are my two favorites.

By now, you will hear many delicious food noises, and this will have made it all worth it!! Days of hard work and preparation will have paid off right then. Smiles all around the table, family together, enjoying each other and the fruits of our labor.

The fun is not over though. After this abundant dinner, there are still desserts to look forward to. Poppy seed cake, ginger bread cookies and my grandma's shortbread cookies are just a few of my favorites. Those will have to wait a bit.

After the dishes have been counted, to make sure everyone had 12, we then open gifts.

Many attend church that night for the midnight mass called "Pasterka", to celebrate the birth of Jesus and sing kolędy (Christmas Carols). Kids love this part. They get to stay up extra late and watch the revealing of the Szopka (Nativity). Very exciting stuff.

Christmas Day

Wigilia – Christmas Eve is followed by, the First and Second Day of Christmas, normally spent with extended family or friends eating, chatting, taking walks, and enjoying each other's company. Meat dishes are added to the mix on the First and Second day of Christmas. Each year we change it up and cook something else. Sometimes a duck or a goose, depending on requests from the family. December 26th is a day when everyone gets sad, because all the pierogi are gone. Each year I tell myself I'm going to make enough and not run out, but that's never the case.

Merry Christmas to you all, my hungry friends. Wishing you a memorable time spent with family, enjoying each other's company, savoring and tasting, being happy and staying healthy.

May the New Year bring a fresh start, new inspirations, new adventures and kindness to one another.

I hope this short book inspires you to spend some time in the kitchen, cooking and sharing with family or friends. I hope these dishes remind you of your Polish family, and restore some long lost flavors. I hope you continue to instill your Polish heritage in your family going forward, and explore many Polish dishes that go beyond gołąbki and kiełbasa... and for those, for whom Polish kitchen is a new territory, welcome to a whole new world of flavors.

With love,
Anna

CHRISTMAS EVE

CHRISTMAS BEETROOT SOUP *Barszcz Wigilijny*

YIELDS: 6-7 SERVINGS | PREP TIME: 5 DAYS | COOK TIME: 30 MIN

Christmas beetroot broth is a savory, lightly sour soup that was made once a year in my home, reserved strictly for Christmas Eve dinner, along with the other 11 dishes served. A small portion of barszcz Wigilijny [bar-sht vee-gee-leey-nih] is served with 4-5 wild mushroom-filled dumplings as the opening dish, warming up everyone's appetite and bringing the traditional tastes of Christmas into the air. Its tangy, earthy and sweet taste is complemented by a mossy and deep flavor of wild mushrooms that cannot be delivered by any other dish that I've ever tasted. It is original and absolutely irresistible.

Ingredients:

STARTER:
» About 1 lbs / 500 g of fresh beets
» 1 tsp of sugar
» 1 tbs of salt
» 4 garlic cloves, crushed
» A piece of rye, pumpernickel or sourdough bread (if you have)
» 1 quart / 4 cups of boiled and cooled water

ADDITIONALLY:
» 2 1/2 cup / 2 oz / 60 g of dried wild mushrooms
» 2 1/2 cups of water
» 1/2 of celery root
» 2 carrots
» 1 celery stalk
» 1 parsnip
» 1/4 of an onion burnt straight on a gas burner
» 1/2 tsp of salt
» 6 each peppercorns and allspice (whole)
» 1/2 cup + 1/2 cup of vinegar (4%)
» 2-3 medium beets
» 1 1/2 tsp of sugar
» 1 tbs of butter
» Sprinkle of dried marjoram
» 3 crushed cloves of garlic

Instructions:

1 Wash, peel and slice your beets into thin slices. Place in a clean glass or ceramic pickling container. Add sugar, salt, garlic, bread and water. Set on the counter for 5 days to sour.

2 One night before you're ready to cook broth, place dried mushrooms in a pot and add 2 1/2 cups of water to soak (make sure it's large enough to fit about 8 cups of liquid). After soaking the mushrooms, add cleaned and peeled celery root, carrots, parsnip, celery stalk, onion, peppercorns, allspice and salt and simmer on low for 20 minutes. Strain the liquid and return it to the pot. Reserve the vegetables.

3 Strain beets that have been souring, add 1/2 cup of vinegar to prevent them from losing rich red color.

4 Clean and peel fresh beets, slice thinly and add to mushroom/vegetable broth. Also add the beets from souring. Simmer for 5 minutes. Remove beets. Add sour beet water to the mushroom/vegetable broth and heat up throughout, but DO NOT BOIL.

5 To finish off, add butter, marjoram and crushed garlic. Taste. If it's too sour/vinegary, add a bit more sugar. Also add a bit more salt, if needed.

A note from <u>Anna</u>:

Beet soup can be difficult to get right, as it loses color fast. Vinegar can help prevent this, but sometimes you may find the soup turning brown. If this happens, don't fret. Even if it loses color this does not affect the taste. Reserve wild mushrooms and vegetables from the broth to make mushroom-filled dumplings (recipe on next page).

MUSHROOM-FILLED SOUP DUMPLINGS *Uszka z Grzybami*

YIELDS: 110 DUMPLINGS | PREP TIME: 4 HRS | COOK TIME: 1.5 HRS

Uszka [oosh-kah] is a plural of the word "ucho" [oo-ho], meaning an ear, most likely due to its shape. Uszka are small dumplings, filled with a wild mushroom and onion mixture. These soft and delicate dumplings are buttery with a strong "woodsy" flavor from the wild mushrooms that are so prominent in the filling. The uszka complete a tart and rich beetroot broth, the opening dish of the Christmas Eve dinner.

Ingredients:

FILLING:
- » 2 1/2 cups / 2 oz / 60 g of dried wild mushrooms
- » 8 oz of baby portobello mushrooms
- » 1 large onion, minced
- » 2 tsp of butter
- » Pinch of salt and pepper

DOUGH:
- » 3 cups of all purpose flour
- » 1 egg
- » 1 tsp of salt
- » 300 ml / 1 1/4 cups of warm water

Instructions:

1 If using wild mushrooms from preparing beet broth (see pg. 18), just place cooked mushrooms in a food processor along with vegetables (carrots, parsnips, celery root) and blend until they're chopped, but not blended into paste.

2 If you're preparing dumplings without making beet broth, soak mushrooms overnight (or for at least 4 hours) in 2 1/2 cups of water, then boil in same water for about 20 minutes. Drain and set aside to cool. Once cooled off, place in a food processor and blend until finely chopped but not blended.

3 Wash baby portobellos and finely chop (or place in a food processor).

4 In a medium skillet heat butter, add minced onion and portobellos, sprinkle with salt. Sauté until cooked and most of liquid has cooked off. Add chopped wild mushrooms and heat through until all liquid has cooked off. Add salt and pepper to taste. Set aside to cool.

5 Prepare dough by combining flour, egg, water and salt. Knead on a floured surface until smooth dough forms.

6 Fill large pot with water, add a splash of oil and about 1 teaspoon of salt and bring to a boil.

7 In batches, roll out dough to about 1/8 of an inch thickness.

8 With a small glass (about 2 inches in diameter), cut out circles. Fill each circle with about a 1/2 teaspoon of mushroom filling. Close each dumpling and press edges with a fork to seal.

9 Once sealed, gently stretch dumpling longways, wrap around one finger and pinch the two pointy ends together to form a round dumpling (resembling an Italian tortellini) - see photos.

10 After dropping into boiling water (in batches of about 20-30), stir gently off the bottom to prevent sticking. Turn heat down to low; water should only be slightly simmering (not rolling boil). When all dumplings float to the top, they are done. Remove from pot and place on a large surface to cool (without touching), or serve right away.

A note from Anna:

This soup develops more flavor with time. It will taste 100% better the next day.

WILD MUSHROOM SOUP

Zupa Grzybowa

YIELDS: 5-6 SMALL SERVINGS | PREP TIME: 4 HRS + 5 MIN | COOK TIME: 25 MIN

Wild mushroom soup is a clear soup, nothing but mushrooms in it. Broth is bold and mushroomy, and lightly creamy. The difference between Christmas mushroom soup [zoo-pah g-rzyh-boh-vah vee-gee-leey-nah] and "regular" mushroom soup is that Christmas mushroom soup is vegetarian. As a matter of fact, all 12 dishes served at Polish Christmas Eve dinner are meatless or made with fish (we don't consider fish meat).

Ingredients:

» 1 oz / 30 g / 1 cup of dried wild mushrooms
» 1 1/2 cups of water for soaking
» 6 cups of vegetable broth (or 6 cups of water and the next 4 ingredients)
» 2 carrots
» 1/2 of celery root
» 1/4 of an onion
» 1 parsnip
» 6 allspice and peppercorns - whole
» 3 bay leaves
» Salt (careful if using broth, it may contain salt already)
» 2 tbs of butter
» 2 tbs of heavy cream

Instructions:

1 Soak wild mushrooms overnight or at least 4 hours.

2 Next day, place mushrooms with the water they were soaking in in a medium pot. Add broth (or water and vegetables), spices and a pinch of salt. Boil covered on low for 30 minutes, or until mushrooms are soft.

3 When wild mushrooms are cooked, strain everything out, reserve the liquid broth. Discard the vegetables (or save to make a Polish vegetable salad), and once the mushrooms cool, dice them and return to broth.

4 Add cream and heat through. Taste, add salt, if needed and a sprinkle of fresh ground pepper. Finish by adding butter for extra flavor.

SAUERKRAUT AND MUSHROOM PIEROGI *Pierogi z Kapustą i z Grzybami*

YIELDS: 60-70 PIEROGI | PREP TIME: 1.5-2 HRS | COOK TIME: 5 MIN

Soft and delicate pierogi dough, and a savory filling, slightly tangy, but not overbearing. You can definitely make out the distinctive nutty and earthy taste of the wild mushrooms. Pierogi z kapustą i z grzybami [pyeh-roh-gee z cap oosow ee z gszyh-bah-mee] is always present on my Christmas table, and even when we think we made plenty, there is never enough.

Ingredients:

FILLING:
- » 27 oz/765 g can of sauer-kraut
- » 8 oz/225 g of baby bella mushrooms
- » 1 oz/30 g of dried shittake mushrooms (or a wild mushroom mix)
- » 1 large onion
- » 1 cup of vegetable broth
- » 1/4 tsp black pepper
- » 2 + 3 tbs of butter

DOUGH:
- » 6 cups of all purpose flour
- » 2 tsp of salt
- » 2 eggs
- » 2 1/2 cup/600 ml of warm water

Instructions:

1. To make the filling you will need to soak dried mushrooms in hot water for at least 1 hour. Boil on low heat for about 20 minutes, or until soft. Drain but reserve the water from boiling. Cool and mince.

2. Heat 2 tablespoons of butter in a large frying pan on medium heat. Add minced onion. In the meantime, shred the portobello mushrooms on the largest vegetable shredder and add to the pan. Sauté until golden brown. Add sauerkraut (liquid and all) to the pan, add mushrooms, vegetable broth, mushroom water and pepper. Heat through and cook uncovered until all liquid evaporates (about 30 minutes). Add remaining butter, stir and cool. The filling is ready!

3. To make the dough, I'm using a kitchen mixer with the hook attachment. My bowl is not that big so I have to split the recipe in half. If you're mixing the dough in a bowl on a surface, feel free to do all at once.

4. If not using a kitchen mixer, place egg and salt in bowl first, whisk lightly. Add flour and water. Mix until ingredients combine and form a dough ball. Take out a portion of it (about a third) onto a floured surface and roll out.

5. With a glass or a pierogi cutter, cut 3 inch circles. Place a tablespoon of filling on each circle and close the dumpling to form a half moon. Pinch edges together, and seal with a fork or your favorite sealing method.

6. Boil in a large pot with a tablespoon of oil and a tablespoon of salt until they all float to the top.

7. Take out and spread on a large plate or surface so they are not touching until cool or serve immediately. You can also brown them in a bit of butter until golden brown.

A note from <u>Anna</u>:

I like to split this task over two days: filling one day, and the rest another day, but it is not necessary. To make this recipe you can use your own home-made sauerkraut, or purchase store-bought. If you decide to go with store-bought, make sure the list of ingredients only includes cabbage and salt. This means kraut soured on its own, without any help from vinegar. Salt (+ time) creates the distinctive tangy taste, vinegar will just make it sour.

CABBAGE WITH YELLOW PEAS

Kapusta z Grochem

YIELDS: 4-6 SERVINGS | PREP TIME: 10 MIN | COOK TIME: 40-50 MIN

Kapusta z grochem [kah-poo-stah z groh-hehm] is often one of the twelve dishes served at Polish Christmas Eve dinner. This dish sometimes gets outshined by other holiday favorites but it, as the others, deserves its own spotlight. It is mild and hearty, with its main flavor component coming from the peas. I like to leave a little crunch to my peas, so they also provide a bit of texture. Cabbage is soft, but also with a little crunch.

Ingredients:

» 1/2 cup of dried yellow peas
» 1/2 tsp salt
» 1 large onion
» 2 tbs of butter/oil
» 1/2 head of cabbage
» 1 cup broth (vegetable, chicken or beef)
» 2 bay leaves
» 4 allspice seeds
» 1 tsp of caraway seed (optional)
» 1/4 tsp ground pepper
» 2 tbs of all purpose flour
» 3 tbs of butter

Instructions:

1 Place raw yellow peas in a pot with 1 1/2 cups of water and 1/2 teaspoon salt and cook on medium heat (covered) for 30 minutes. I like mine with just a little bit of substance, so I don't boil them until they fall apart.

2 In the mean time, cut cabbage in half and thinly slice one half in a shredder or hand slice. Chop into smaller pieces. Chop 1 onion, and sauté with bay leaves, allspice and caraway seeds in butter until golden brown in a medium/large pot (cabbage will join in).

3 When onions are ready, add cabbage and broth and cook uncovered for about 10 minutes to soften the cabbage. Add peas, and mix well to combine.

4 In a small pan make roux by melting butter and adding flour, add to cabbage and stir in. Taste, add more salt, if needed. Add ground pepper at the end.

CABBAGE WITH WILD *Kapusta z Grzybami* MUSHROOMS

YIELDS: 6-7 SERVINGS | PREP TIME: 20 MIN | COOK TIME: 1.5 HRS + 1.5 HRS

Kapusta z grzybami [kah-poos-tah z gshi-bah-mee] is a vegetarian version of bigos, by Poles often called "bigos jarski". It is prepared with both fresh cabbage and sauerkraut, dried wild mushrooms and fresh mushrooms and spices. It's tangy and aromatic, and fills my kitchen with smells of the home I grew up in. We always make this dish for our Christmas Eve feast, as it fits with the no-meat rules.

Ingredients:

» 1/2 head of cabbage
» 1 can (14 oz / 500 g) of sauerkraut
» 1 1/2 cups of water
» 3 bay leaves
» 6 peppercorns (whole) and allspice each
» 1 tsp salt
» 16 - 20 oz / 500 - 700 g of baby bellas / button mushrooms
» 1 large onion, chopped
» About 1 cup of dried mushrooms*
» 2 tbs of tomato paste

Instructions:

1 Place dried mushrooms in a small pot, add enough boiling water to cover, set aside until mushrooms rehydrate (best to do this overnight).

2 Shred cabbage and cut into smaller pieces. Place in a large pot with 1 1/5 cups of water, bay leaves, peppercorns, allspice and salt. Boil on medium heat until cabbage softens (only about 5 minutes). Add sauerkraut (I don't drain my sauerkraut, nor do I rinse it. If you like your kraut a bit milder, rinse it). Continue cooking on medium-low.

3 Clean and slice button mushrooms. Sauté in butter until golden brown around the edges. Transfer to cabbage mixture. Sauté chopped onion (add a bit more butter if needed), and add it to the party.

4 After dried mushrooms rehydrate, boil them for about 10 minutes on low (check if they're soft, if not, boil for a bit longer. Add more water if needed). When mushrooms are soft, dump the water from boiling them into cabbage mixture. Chop wild mushrooms and add to the cabbage also.

5 Add tomato paste and continue cooking for total cooking time of about 1 hour. Turn off and set aside to cool. Refrigerate overnight. Next day, cook again for another hour and a half or so.

6 This dish does well in the fridge and tastes best if cooked over several days. Give it at least two days (1.5 hours each day) of cooking before serving, for best results.

28

A note from <u>Anna:</u>

*Wild mushrooms should not be served to small children. Do your research before serving to anyone under 12 years old.

A note from <u>Anna:</u>

Although this dish is served cold during Christmas, it
does well and tastes great served as a hot entrée.

GREEK STYLE FISH *Ryba Po Grecku*

YIELDS: 5-6 SERVINGS | PREP TIME: 10 MIN | COOK TIME: 30 MIN

Ryba po grecku [ryh-bah poh greh-tskoo] is a traditional Polish Christmas dish, and not, as one may think, a Greek dish. It is unknown where the name of this dish came from, but it is assumed that it relates to the cooking method. Greeks, due to the geographical location, eat a lot of fish and seafood, a lot of times prepared and served with stewed vegetables in season. Perhaps Poles, by using a similar cooking method, decided to call it "Greek style" fish at some point, but that's the only resemblance to Greek food.

Ingredients:

» 1 lb / 500 g of fish filets (any white, mild fish will do)
» 1 egg
» 3 tbs of flour
» 3-4 tbs of oil
» 5 carrots
» 1 parsnip
» 1/2 medium celery root or 3/4 of a small one
» 1 1/2 cups of chopped onion
» 1 tbs of oil + 1 tbs of butter
» 1/2 cup of vegetable broth or water
» 3 tbs of tomato paste
» 1 tsp salt
» Sprinkle of pepper
» 3 bay leaves
» 6 peppercorns and allspice each (whole)
» 2 tsp paprika

Instructions:

1 Wash fish filets and pat dry and cut into smaller pieces (about 3 inch/7cm). Sprinkle with salt and pepper. Break an egg into one dish, add a tablespoon of water and whisk. Place flour in another dish. Heat oil in a non-stick frying pan. Dredge each piece of fish in egg and flour and sauté on medium until cooked and lightly brown. Remove and place on a paper towel.

2 Peel carrots, parsnip and celery root and shred on a course vegetable shredder. Chop onion. Heat oil and butter in a wide pan/deep frying pan and add peppercorns, allspice and bay leaves, followed by shredded vegetables and onions. Heat through. Add broth, tomato sauce, salt and pepper and paprika. Sauté until cooked, about 5-7 minutes. Don't overcook, leave a bit of crunch in the veggies.

3 Taste. Add a bit more salt, if needed.

4 Once veggies are cooked, create layers in a deep serving dish by placing about 1/3 of the veggie mixture first, then arrange fish pieces and cover with the rest of the veggie mixture. Cover with foil and let cool. Refrigerate until serving.

37

FRIED CARP
Karp

PREP TIME: 2 HRS | COOK TIME: 20 MIN

Carp is an oily freshwater fish that tastes briny and mildly fishy, soft and flaky. It will be lightly sautéed in an oil and butter mixture for a thin golden brown crust. It is a national treasure here in Poland and is always served on Christmas Eve.

Ingredients:

» 2 lbs of carp (or other large whole fish, like striped bass)
» Salt
» Pepper
» 4 tbs of flour
» 3 tbs of oil
» 2 tbs of butter

Instructions:

1 Clean and wash fish. Cut head and tail off.

2 Cut fish into steaks, as shown in photo.

3 Place fish in a bowl, add 2 tablespoons of salt, cover with cold water and refrigerate for 2 hours.

4 Remove, rinse and pat dry.

5 Sprinkle with pepper. Place flour in a shallow dish or a plastic bag. Add fish pieces to lightly coat. Shake off any excess flour.

6 In a large frying pan, heat oil and butter. Place pieces of fish and sauté for a few minutes on each side on medium heat. Remove and place on a paper towel to soak up extra fat. If steaks are thick, finish in a 350°F / 180°C oven for a few minutes to cook through.

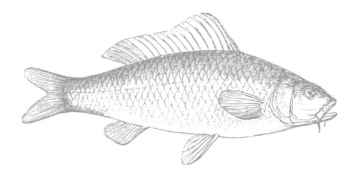

A note from <u>Anna</u>:

Serve immediatly or keep in a warm oven until ready to serve.

A note from <u>Anna</u>:

* The proper way of making this dish is with salted herring filets, called "herring a la Matias" — most Polish delis carry those. If you are unable to find those, however, use pickled herring in wine sauce. The salted herring is made by curing in salt only. Salt "cooks" it and it's then stored in oil. The process also softens the fish bones, so no need to worry about deboning. Pickled herring on the other hand is preserved with vinegar and spices, therefore the two have slightly different taste.

HERRING IN SOUR CREAM Śledź w Śmietanie

YIELDS: 4 SERVINGS | PREP TIME: 10 MIN | COOK TIME: 10 MIN

I know, you're already thinking this can't work... I admit, it seems this one is for more adventurous eaters, but if you like fish, you will like this rendition of a very under-appreciated (in America) piece of fish. The combination of hot potatoes and cold, sweet and crunchy mixture of onion, apple and salty, fishy taste of herring makes this dish unusual but very satisfying. It just works.

Ingredients:

- » About 7 oz (1 cup) of salted herring (a la matias)*
- » 1 large onion
- » 1 apple
- » 1 cup of sour cream
- » 3-5 potatoes
- » Pinch of pepper

Instructions:

1 Cut the onion in a half and slice each half. Place slices in a strainer and run a pot of freshly boiled water through the onions to make them slightly softer and more mild.

2 Drain the herring and cut into bite size pieces. Place in a mixing bowl.

3 Once the onions have cooled, shred the apple on a course side of the grater and add both to the fish.

4 Add sour cream immediately, to prevent the apple from turning brown. Add pepper and mix well.

5 Cover and cool in the fridge for at least an hour.

6 When ready to serve, boil peeled potatoes. Place hot potatoes on a plate and top with the cold fish mixture.

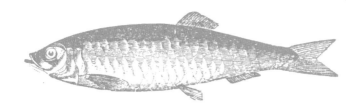

HERRING IN OIL
Śledź w oleju

Herring does have a pretty robust flavor, even for pretty die-hard fish lovers, but in this case, paired with a fragrant onion, it becomes more mild and quite palatable.

Ingredients:

» 8-9 oz/250 g of salted herring
» 1 medium onion, thinly sliced
» 1 cup of vegetable oil (I like canola)
» 1/4 tsp of granulated sugar
» 1/4 tsp of ground pepper, freshly ground if possible
» 1/2 cup of chopped parsley

Instructions:

1 Drain herring and set on paper towels to dry a bit.

2 Cut onion in half and slice thinly. Place in a bowl.

3 Add oil, sugar, pepper and chopped parsley.

4 Slice herring at an angle into about 1 inch / 3 cm strips. Add to bowl.

5 Mix and refrigerate for at least 1 hour.

A note from <u>Anna:</u>

The proper way of making this dish is with salted herring filets, called "herring a la Matias" — most Polish delis carry those. The salted herring is made by curing in salt only. Salt "cooks" it and it's then stored in oil. The process also softens the fish bones, so no need to worry about deboning. Pickled herring on the other hand is preserved with vinegar and spices, therefore the two have slightly different taste.

FISH ASPIC
Ryba w Galarecie

YIELDS: 6 (1/2CUP) SERVINGS | PREP TIME: 30 MIN | COOK TIME: 45 MINS

Ryba w galarecie [ryh-bah v gah-lah-reh-chye] is a mild and well seasoned fish dish. Fish/gelatin broth is savory and lightly garlicky, with pieces of soft fish, boiled eggs and carrots bringing a bit of extra texture. This dish is primarily made for Christmas Eve dinner in my home.

Ingredients:

» About 1 lb / 500 g fish parts (head, tail, fins)
» 3 carrots
» 1 parsnip
» 1/2 of celery root or 1 celery stalk
» 1/4 of an onion burnt directly on the gas burner
» 3 bay leaves
» 4-5 peppercorns and allspice (each)
» 4 cups of water
» 1 tsp of salt
» 2 filets of a mild white fish (about 10 oz / 300 g)
» 5 envelopes of gelatin (40 g)
» 2 garlic cloves
» 2-3 sprigs of fresh dill
» 1 hard-boiled egg
» 1/2 cup of frozen or canned peas

Instructions:

1 Place fish parts and the next 8 ingredients in a soup pot and boil on low for 30 min. Strain broth, remove and discard all but the carrots. Return broth to the pot. Add fish filets and simmer on low for about 10 minutes (until fish is cooked). Remove fish gently and cool.

2 Boil egg and thinly slice. Slice carrots.

3 While broth is still hot add gelatin by slowly pouring powder into the hot soup and whisking vigorously. Crush dill sprigs in between your fingers and add to broth/gelatin mixture, along with crushed garlic cloves. Leave for 15 minutes. Remove dill and garlic.

4 Place 6 glass containers (mine are about 1/2 cup each)onto a tray. Place a slice of an egg, carrot slices, a few peas into each container. Then place pieces of cooked fish filets (evenly divide between all containers) - see photo.

5 Gently pour fish broth over fish and vegetables to cover. Transfer tray into the fridge and cool overnight.

6 Serve with bread, sprinkled with lemon juice or white vinegar. Horseradish is also a great condiment for the dish.

POPPY SEEDS WITH DUMPLINGS
Kluski z Makiem

YIELDS: 6-10 SERVINGS | PREP TIME: 1 HR | COOK TIME: 10 MIN

Kluski z makiem [cloo-skee z mah-kyem] is a sweet mixture of pasta-like dumplings, called łazanki [wah-zah-nkee], cooked poppy seeds, sweet honey, raisins and nuts. This classic dish, has a "sister" dish, called "kutia" made from boiled wheat grain instead of dumplings. In my house however, we always made łazanki for Christmas.

Ingredients:

» 2/3 cup / 100 g / 4 oz of raisins
» 7 oz / 200 g of raw poppy seeds*
» 1 cup / 250 ml of water
» 3 tbs of honey
» Pinch of salt
» 2 tbs of butter
» 1 cup / 100 g / 4 oz of walnuts, chopped

» DUMPLINGS:
» 1 1/2 cups / 200 g of all purpose flour
» 1 egg
» 1/2 -2/3 cup (100-150 ml) of warm water

Instructions:

1 Place raisins in a container and cover with warm water. Set aside to soak.

2 Place poppy seeds in a medium boiling pot and add enough warm water to cover, set aside to soak for about 10 minutes, then boil for 20-25 minutes. Add a bit more water, if they get dry, enough to cover. After 25 minutes, drain well.

3 Fill a medium-large pot with water, add a splash of oil and a teaspoon of salt and bring to boil.

4 In the mean time, make dumplings by combining all ingredients in a mixing bowl of a stand up mixer and mix with a hook attachment. If you are working by hand, mix all ingredients in a mixing bowl.

5 When combined, transfer onto a clean, floured surface (preferably a large cutting board) and knead until smooth. Roll out with a rolling pin and cut into strips (a pizza cutter works great!) and then diagonally (see photo).

6 Sprinkle dumplings with flour and, with the help of your knife lift them off of your surface, so they do not stick together (see photo). When water is boiling, slide them off your cutting board into the pot and IMMEDIATELY stir gently, we don't want them clumping together. Turn heat down and let simmer until dumplings float to the top. Drain and set aside to cool.

7 Now, we will work on the poppy seeds. Once they cool slightly you will have to put them through a meat grinder with the fine grinding plate – TWICE.

8 Once you've done that place ground poppy seeds in a medium pot, add water (1 cup / 250 ml), honey and a pinch of salt, and also water from soaking raisins. Simmer on low until water evaporates. Lastly, add butter and stir to melt and incorporate.

9 Transfer poppy seed mixture to a large bowl, add raisins, walnuts and dumplings. Mix to combine. Dish can be served cold or warm.

A note from Anna:

*you can use poppy seed cake filling (called "masa makowa" available at most Polish stores in the US or on line, link here). If you are using the canned filling, you will need about half of the can (about 450 g), and won't have to add any nuts or honey, filling is ready to go!

A note from Anna:
Fruit are also eaten as a dessert, but normally there is some left. I normally put the remaining uneaten fruit into a food processor and blend until smooth (remember to remove spices before doing this). We eat this delicious blended dried fruit jam as jelly on toast, add it to oat-meal or smear over pancakes.

DRIED FRUIT JUICE

Kompot z Suszu

YIELDS: 6-10 SERVINGS | PREP TIME: 1 HR | COOK TIME: 30 MIN

Kompot z suszu [kohm-poht z soo-shoo] is a sweet and fragrant juice made from dried fruit and spices only, no sugar added. Despite that fact, it can be very sweet. I normally dilute it to get it to the level of sweetness I like. Kompot is ALWAYS present at Christmas and I don't know anyone who does not like, or make it for the holidays. It is solely made for the occasion so the flavor immediately puts me in a Christmas spirit.

Ingredients:

» 2 cups of dried fruit - apples, prunes, mango, raisins, cranberries, pears
» 2 cinnamon sticks
» 5 cloves
» 6 cups of water

Instructions:

1 Place all ingredients in a pot and boil on low for 30 minutes.

2 Store overnight.

3 Next day, taste and dilute to desired sweetness.

CHRISTMAS
DAY

Traditions

Christmas Eve is normally spent with immediate family: children, parents, siblings and grandparents. Christmas Day will be celebrated with extended family and friends. We gather around a set table, and usually end up staying there for most of the day.

The Catholic Church will host a mass, and an afternoon walk will provide room for more food later.

We also exchange small gifts with our guests, such as a box of home-made cookies, chocolates or a small trinquet. Afterall, it's not about the gifts, but the memories that come with being together.

Menu

Christmas Day is a whole other story as far as the menu goes. We are no longer restricted by "no-meat" rule, so sky is the limit. There are however, a few dishes that come to mind, which are prepared for special occasions: Christmas, someone's big birthday, First Communion, and such.

I'm presenting a few suggestions for Christmas Day dinner, paired with a few classic dishes that traditionally go well with them.

Dishes from Christmas Eve dinner may be served (if there are any left) but often a "new" course will be presented.

First and foremost, chicken soup is usually present at every family gathering. It is a solid must-have on my family table! I will also serve duck blood soup for the traditionalists and foodies in my family.

Goose legs are a good option, and will go well with Silesian potato dumplings and fried red cabbage, and roasted duck is almost always served with fried beets.

For the less adventurous eaters, I suggest stuffed chicken. A side of dumplings or boiled potatoes will complement this dish, and a side of beets or another cold salad will complete it.

I wish you the best of luck creating your Christmas menu. I hope you find something that fits your family table.

Smacznego!

A note from <u>Anna:</u>

No cutting corners here and using boxed broth. If you want this to work, you gotta go full in and do it right. Get the fresh veggies, prepare the broth and the results will knock you off your feet.
* If you have a hard time finding blood, just omit it. The flavor mainly comes from the duck and fruit.

DUCK BLOOD SOUP
Czernina

YIELDS: 6-8 SERVINGS | PREP TIME: 15 MIN | COOK TIME: ABOUT 2 HRS

Duck blood soup is an "old school" delicacy. Recipe for this traditional soup was passed down from generation to generation and, in my family, it has not changed for at least 4 generations. The end result will deliver a very mild, slightly sweet but also savory broth with hints of fruit. The very distinct flavor comes from the duck meat, not the blood. Very little blood added to it gives the chocolate color but only a little bit of flavor.

Ingredients:

» 1 duck - we'll use breast bones, neck and giblets only
» 3 carrots
» 1 parsnip
» 1/2 of small leek
» 1/4 of a small celery root and a few twigs of the leafy part
» 1/4 of an onion, burnt over a gas stove or on a dry pan
» 6 peppercorns and allspice each (whole)
» 3-4 bay leaves
» 1 tbs of salt
» 7 cups / 1 1/2 liters of water
» 4-5 dried mushrooms
» 1/2 cup of dried apples
» 10 prunes
» 1/4 cup of dried pears
» 1 cup of home-made canned tart cherries, plus 1 cup of cherry juice (or 1 - 14.5 oz / 400 g can of tart cherries)
» 1 tbs of all purpose flour
» 1 cup / 230 ml of cold water
» About 3/4 cup / 180-200 ml of duck blood*
» 1 tbs of vinegar
» Additional salt
» 1/2-1 tsp of sugar

Instructions:

1 Place dried fruit and mushrooms in 2 cups / 450 ml of water overnight or for at least 1 hour.

2 Wash the duck, remove wings, breasts and legs leaving the breast bone, neck and gizzards to make a flavorful broth. If this is too difficult of a task, ask your butcher for help.

3 Place meat, carrots and vegetables in a medium pot and add water, salt, peppercorns, allspice and bay leaves. Boil on low heat for 1.5 hours. Remove meat and veggies from the pot and strain the broth.

4 Place broth back on heat. Add reconstituted fruit, mushrooms and tart cherries. Simmer on low for about 10 minutes.

5 In the meantime, mix flour with cold water well (no clumps). Mix blood with vinegar and add to water/flour mixture. Pour into soup, and bring to boil. Turn off. Taste, add a bit of salt and sugar, if needed. Amount of sugar will depend on the level of sweetness in dried fruit and cherries. Soup should be slightly sweet and savory. Vinegar is not a super prevalent flavor in it. Add salt and sugar bit by bit to get to the desired flavor.

6 Serve over thin egg noodles or thin (angel hair) spaghetti.

A note from <u>Anna</u>:

*If you are serving chicken soup as the main course, add chicken meat to the broth. If it is only a starter, save the meat for another day and serve with just noodles and carrots, garnished with fresh parsley.

CHICKEN SOUP
Rosót

YIELDS: 10 SERVINGS | PREP TIME: 10 MIN | COOK TIME: ABOUT 1-1.5 HRS

Chicken soup is a mild but flavorful soup made with fresh whole chicken, fresh vegetables and served with thin egg noodles. It is nothing like the broth you get at the store and it is worth the time and effort. It always reminds me of my home and will be a great addition to a traditional Polish Christmas.

Ingredients:

» 1 good quality whole chicken
» 3 carrots
» 1 parsnip
» 1/2 of a celery root
» 1/4 of an onion
» 1-2 dried Polish wild mushrooms (or shiitake mushrooms)
» A few sprigs of green parsley
» 4 bay leaves
» 6 allspice, whole
» 6 peppercorns, whole
» Salt
» Favorite pasta (preferably thin egg pasta or angel hair spaghetti)

Instructions:

1 Wash chicken and vegetables and place in a large pot. Add salt, spices and mushrooms. Fill with water to cover meat.

2 Place onion on an open flame of a gas burner and burn both sides of the cut quarter. If cooking on electric stove, place onion in a dry frying pan, until burnt. Add to the mix.

3 Cover the pot and simmer on low for about 1-1.5 hours.

4 When chicken is tender and falls off the bone, remove and take off the bone.*

5 Fill each serving bowl with a few scoops of boiled pasta (I like the thin egg noodles or angel hair pasta), add a few slices of carrot, as much meat as you'd like and garnish with a pinch of chopped parsley. Fill bowl with liquid and enjoy!

A note from <u>Anna</u>:

Save leftover goose fat for frying, it's delicious.
Strain out apples and pears, and store fat in a jar in
the fridge.

ROASTED GOOSE LEGS *Gęsie Nogi*

YIELDS: 1 LEG PER PERSON | PREP TIME: 10 MIN + OVERNIGHT | COOK TIME: 2.5-3HRS

Polish geese are famous in Europe for their delicate meat. They are relatively easy to find; most large grocery stores will have a stock in the freezer section. I'm roasting goose legs "gęsie nogi" [gew-shye no-ghee] only, as I think the leg meat is the most delicious. Goose meat is super fatty. Long roasting allows the fat to soak into the tough meat, making it super tender, moist and full of flavor.

Ingredients:

» Goose legs
» Salt and pepper
» Fresh thyme or marjoram
» About 1/2 of an apple and 1/2 of a pear per leg

Instructions:

1 Wash and dry goose legs. Sprinkle with salt and pepper and herbs. Place in the fridge overnight.

2 Preheat oven to 300°F / 150°C.

3 Wash apples and pears. Cut them into quarters, remove seeds. Place fruit on the bottom of a roasting pan and then goose legs on top of the fruit.

4 Roast for 2.5-3 hours, basting occasionally.

5 When ready, take out of the oven, cover with a kitchen towel and rest for 15 minutes before serving.

A note from <u>Anna:</u>

After baking, let chicken rest (covered) for
5 minutes.

BUCKWHEAT STUFFED CHICKEN

Kurczak Nadziewany Kaszą Gryczaną

YIELDS: 4 SERVINGS | PREP TIME: 30 MIN | COOK TIME: 50-60 MINS

Chicken stuffed with buckwheat, mushrooms and walnuts. This is a dinner dish that will take ordinary to extraordinary with just a few classic Polish ingredients.

Ingredients:

» 1 whole chicken (mine was about 1400 g / 3 lbs)
» 1 1/2 cups of cooked buckwheat
» 1 tsp of salt
» 200 g / 7 oz of fresh button mushrooms
» 1 medium onion
» 1 oz / 30 g / 2 tbs of butter + 2 oz / 55 g / 4 tbs of butter
» 4 garlic cloves
» 1 tsp of ground pepper
» 8-10 twigs of fresh dill
» 1/3 cup of chopped walnuts

Instructions:

1 Wash and dry the chicken. Set aside at room temperature.

2 Prepare buckwheat according to instructions on the package with 1/2 teaspoon of salt. Once cooked, transfer to a large mixing bowl and set aside.

3 In the meantime, wash and dice mushrooms and onion. In a medium skillet, heat 1 oz / 30 g / 2 tablespoons of butter, add mushrooms, onions, 2 cloves of chopped garlic, 1/4 teaspoon ground pepper, 1/2 teaspoon of salt and sauté until golden brown (for about 10 minutes). Transfer to the bowl with buckwheat. Also add chopped dill and walnuts. Mix well and taste. Add a bit more salt and pepper, if needed.

4 In a small skillet on low heat, melt 2 oz / 55 g / 4 tablespoons of butter, add 2 cloves of garlic, 1/2 teaspoon of salt and 1/4 teaspoon (or more if you like spicy) of ground pepper.

5 Preheat oven to 350°F / 180°C.

6 Prepare a baking/roasting dish. Place chicken in it and pour 1 tablespoon of melted butter into the cavity and distribute around it. Spoon stuffing into the cavity, pushing firmly. Portion of your stuffing will be exposed, that's OK.

7 Once stuffed, brush/pour the rest of the melted butter on top of the bird evenly. Bake uncovered for 50-60 minutes, or until internal temperature reaches 160°F / 75°C. I basted mine twice during the baking, but it's not mandatory.

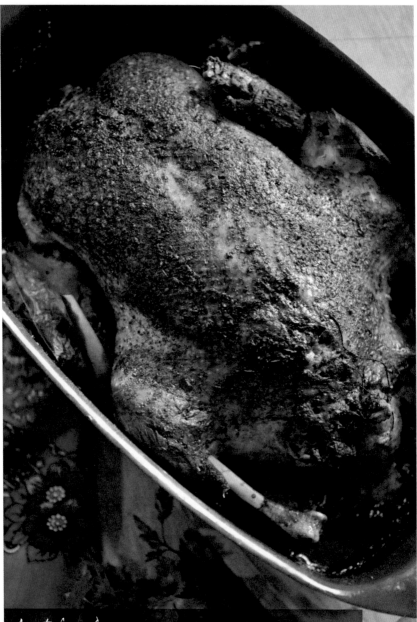

A note from Anna:

* If you are not into liver and/or gizzards, stuff with fresh apples and pears. Wash apples and pears, quarter them and place in duck cavity, no need to sew duck, in this case.

ROASTED DUCK
Kaczka Pieczona

YIELDS: 5-6 SERVINGS | PREP TIME: 30 MIN | COOK TIME: 2.5-3 HRS

Traditional Polish roasted duck, kaczka pieczona [cah-chkah pyeh-choh-nah], stuffed with a mixture of livers and gizzards, the most traditional way of preparing duck, as far as I know. This is a method I learned from my grandma Stasia, who was born and grew up in central Poland, the small village of Oraczew Wielki, right outside Sieradz. Roasted duck is normally prepared for special ocassions in Poland, and it will represent your Polish heritage proudly.

Ingredients:

» 1 duck
» 1 tbs of salt
» 2 tsp of freshly ground pepper
» 1 tbs of dried marjoram

STUFFING*:
» 10 oz / 30 g of chicken and/or duck livers
» 10 oz / 30 g of chicken and/or duck gizzards
» 1 kaiser roll
» 3 whole eggs
» 4 oz / 100 g of butter
» 3 tbs of fresh parsley
» 2 tsp of salt
» 2 tsp of pepper

» ADDITIONALLY:
» Needle and a natural thread for sewing up the duck

Instructions:

1 Rinse duck and pat dry. Sprinkle with salt, pepper and marjoram. Leave out of the fridge to bring to room temperature.

2 Rinse livers and gizzards, set aside to drain. Place kaiser roll in a container with a cup of water, let it soak it up.

3 Put livers and gizzards through a meat grinder, at the end, squeeze water out of the kaiser roll and also put through the grinder.

4 To the stuffing mixture, add eggs, diced butter, chopped parsley, salt, pepper and mix until well combined.

5 Preheat oven to 350°F / 180°C.

6 Prepare needle and thread. Place duck in a baking dish. Spoon stuffing into the duck, fill as much as you can. Fold ducktail up and sew up with the needle and thread to close the cavity. It doesn't have to be pretty, the idea is to keep the stuffing from flowing out.

7 COVER baking dish and bake 2.5-3 hours (about 30 minutes per pound / about 1 hour per kilo). Baste with juices that duck produces about every hour. Take cover off for the last 20 minutes and let the bird brown.

BEEF STEAKS IN MUSTARD SAUCE

Bitki Wołowe w Sosie Musztardowym

YIELDS: 5-6 SERVINGS | PREP TIME: 10 MIN | COOK TIME: 2 HRS

Bitki Wołowe w Sosie Musztardowym [beet-kee vo-wo-veh v soh-sheh moo-shtar-doh-vim] are beef cutlets, simmered until they are soft and tender, in an aromatic brown mustard sauce served over a favorite starch. This decadent cut of beef will make your holiday dinner special and satisfying.

Ingredients:

» 1 eye round roast (mine was about 1lb 13 oz / 800 g) or other lean beef roast
» 2 - 3 tbs of oil
» 4 cups of stock (beef, chicken or vegetable)
» 3 bay leaves
» 6 allspice seeds
» A few sprigs of thyme (if have on hand)
» 3 garlic cloves, crushed
» 1 tsp of salt
» Salt and pepper
» 3 tbs of butter
» 3 tbs of flour
» 4 tbs of brown mustard

Instructions:

1 Wash and dry beef roast. With a large sharp knife slice 3/4 inch thick steaks. With a meat tenderizer pound them out to about 1/2 inch / 1.5 cm thickness. Sprinkle each steak with salt and pepper.

2 In a medium skillet heat oil and sauté beef for a few minutes on each side, until a little brown. Transfer to a medium pan, add stock (if using low sodium stock, add a teaspoon of salt), bay leaf, all spice, thyme, garlic and simmer (covered) on low for about 2 hours (until meat is tender).

3 Gently take steaks out, and set aside (you don't want to whisk the sauce with the beef in the pot, it may break apart).

4 In a small pan make roux: heat butter until bubbly, add flour and stir until lightly brown (about 2 minutes). Add a little bit of the stock from beef into the roux, whisk and heat through. Add mustard and whisk until combined.

5 Transfer roux into sauce and stir well. Bring to boil. Sauce will thicken. Taste. Add salt, if needed and a sprinkle of freshly ground pepper. Return beef steaks into the sauce. Serve hot.

SILESIAN POTATO DUMPLINGS

Kluski Śląskie

YIELDS: 30 DUMPLINGS | PREP TIME: 20 MIN | COOK TIME: 10 MINS

Kluski śląskie z dziurką, [kloo-ski shlon-skieh z dgoor-koh] means Silesian dumplings with a hole. Their name suggests they originated in Silesia region of Poland, which is located in the South-West part of the country. They are a mild dumpling, slightly rubbery, but still soft, ready to soak up warm gravy. They are a must-have side dish when serving duck or goose.

Ingredients:

- » 2 lbs / 1 kg of raw potatoes
- » 1/2 cup of potato flour (or corn starch)
- » 1/2 cup of all purpose flour
- » 1/2 tsp of salt

Instructions:

1 Wash, peel and boil potatoes in salted water.

2 Fill a large pot with water, add a teaspoon of salt and a splash of oil. Set to boil.

3 When potatoes are soft, drain and while still hot transfer to a bowl. With an electric hand mixer mix potatoes for about 1 minute until all broken apart (you can use a hand masher also). Add flours and salt and blend for another 20 seconds.

4 Transfer dough to a clean surface and fold until a dough ball forms. Cut a piece off, roll out a thick log, cut log into pieces about 1 inch / 3 cm long. Roll each piece in your hands to form a ball. Flatten the ball slightly. With handle of a knife or a spatula, make an indentation in the dumpling (see photos).

5 Once water is boiling, add dumplings (I did mine in 2 batches), and simmer on low for about 1 minute from the time they float to the top. Don't overdo this part. They will start falling apart, if boiled too long.

6 Remove and lay out on a cookie sheet (without touching), or serve immediately.

A note from Anna:

If reheating, submerge in boiling water for a minute or two.

A note from Anna:

To reheat, place in a pan with butter, brown on all sides or place in hot water bath for a few minutes.

POTATO DUMPLINGS
Kopytka

YIELDS: 6-10 SERVINGS | PREP TIME: 15 MIN | COOK TIME: 4 MINS

Soft and doughy potato dumplings made from cooked potatoes, egg and flour only. A simple but satisfying dish that goes well with even the most sofisticated dinner, like goose legs or roasted duck.

Ingredients:

» 1 lb / 500 g of cooked and cooled potatoes (leftovers are great!)
» 1 egg
» 1 cup of all purpose flour
» 1 tsp of salt

Instructions:

1 Fill a large pot with water, salt it with a teaspoon of salt, and add a tablespoon of oil.

2 Mash potatoes with a potato masher in a pot. Add remaining ingredients, and mix to form a pliable dough, transfer onto floured surface, to make it easier to work with. Cut a thick slice of dough and roll out on a flat surface gently sprinkled with flour, to form a long roll.

3 Cut it into 1 inch / 3 cm pieces at a 45-degree angle.

4 Place raw dumplings in boiling water in batches (I did this in 2 batches in a 6 quart pot), stir gently to prevent dumplings from sticking to the bottom and to each other. Simmer on low for about 1 minute from the time they start floating to the top (about 3 minute total). Remove from water and lay out on a cookie sheet (so they don't stick together). Serve hot.

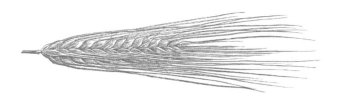

A note from <u>Anna:</u>

To reheat, place in a pan with butter, brown on all sides or place in hot water bath for a few minutes.

POTATO & PUMPKIN DUMPLINGS

Kopytka Dyniowe

An updated version of traditional "kopytka", this potato dumpling also incorporates a favorite fall and winter vegetable: pumpkin. Combine this with any protein and gravy and you have a comfort-food like dish. Kopytka dyniowe [koh-pit-kah dyh-nyo-veh] are starchy and slightly rubbery, they make a great vehicle for a warm and smooth gravy.

Ingredients:

» 1 1/2 lbs / 4 cups of boiled and mashed potatoes
» 2 eggs
» 15 oz / 425 g can of pumpkin puree
» 2 tsp of salt
» 3 cups of all purpose flour
» Splash of oil

Instructions:

1 Place potatoes, pumpkin purée, eggs and salt in a large bowl and mash with a hand potato masher until combined. Small lumps of potatoes may be visible.

2 Add flour in 1/2 cup increments, and combine with your hands to form dough.

3 Fill a large pot with water, add about 1 tablespoon of salt and a splash of oil and bring to boil.

4 In the mean time, take a portion of the dough and place on a surface sprinkled with flour. Form a log and start rolling against the surface with your hands with an outward motion until the roll is about 1 inch / 3 cm in diameter. With a sharp knife cut dough at a 45° angle into the shape of a rhombus.

5 When water reaches boiling temperature start dropping dumplings into the water in batches. Boil on medium–low heat until they float to the top. Remove and spread on a cookie sheets or other surface to cool or serve immediately.

FRIED RED CABBAGE WITH APPLES

Czerwona Kapusta z Jabłkami

YIELDS: 8-10 SERVINGS | PREP TIME: 10 MIN | COOK TIME: 15 MINS

This red-headed sister of beloved green cabbage in this dish is sweet and fruity with a crunch. Apple provides nice sweetness to it and the roux makes it creamy. This fried red cabbage with apples [chehr-voh-nah kap-poos-tah z jabw-kah-mee] dish breaks up the rich flavor of the meat and joins the two in a perfect marriage of savory and sweet, crunchy and creamy.

Ingredients:

» 1 head of red cabbage (about 2 lbs / 1 kg)
» 1 apple
» 1 tsp salt
» 1 1/2 cups / 350 ml of water
» 4 tbs / 55 g of butter
» 3 tbs of flour
» 1/4 cup / 60 ml of vinegar (4%)
» 1/2 tsp of sugar
» 2 bay leaves
» 4 allspice berries
» 4 peppercorns whole

Instructions:

1 Cut cabbage into quarters and shred by hand or using a mandolin. Place in a medium pot with water and salt and heat through only until it wilts a bit (about 5-7 minutes).

2 Wash, peel and core the apple and shred it on the course side of a grater.

3 In a separate pot melt butter. Add flour and brown for about 30 seconds, add cabbage with liquid. Add vinegar, allspice berries, shredded apple and sugar and stir. Cook over medium heat until water evaporates stirring occasionally (about 15 minutes). Cabbage should become softer, but keep the crunch.

67

A note from <u>Anna</u>:

Roast beets a day or two ahead, to save time.
Never use store-bought canned beets, they
do not compare!

FRIED BEETS
Buraczki Zasmażane

YIELDS: 3-4 (1/2 CUP) SERVINGS | PREP TIME: 1HR (ROASTING) | COOK TIME: 10 MINS

Buraczki zasmażane [boo-rach-kee zah-smah-rgah-neh], warm and creamy beets, slightly sweet and tangy make a great addition to a rich dinner of goose or duck.

Ingredients:

» 3 medium beets
» 2 tbs of butter
» 2 tbs of flour
» 1/2 tsp sugar
» 1/4 cup of cream
» 3 tbs of white vinegar
» Pinch of salt

Instructions:

1 Preheat oven to 350°F / 180°C. Wash beets and roast in the oven (covered) for about 1 hour (until soft).

2 Remove from oven and cool.

3 Peel and grate on the finest vegetable grater (yep, the one that takes finger tips off - CAREFUL!)

4 In a medium pan, heat butter on low heat, add flour to make roux. Stir until combined and bubbly, about 30 seconds.

5 Add grated beets and the rest of the ingredients, heat through. Taste and add a bit more salt, if needed.

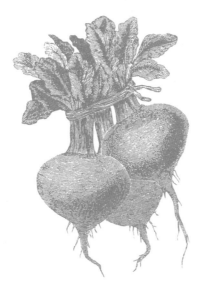

A note from <u>Anna:</u>

*Mix salad well before serving.
You may roast the beets a day ahead. It will cut
down on cooking time the day of.

BEETROOT SALAD
Surówka z buraczków

YIELDS: 4 SERVINGS | PREP TIME: 1HR (ROASTING) | COOK TIME: 15 MINS

Beets, my (and most of Poland's) comfort food, surówka z buraczków [soo-roov-kah z boo-rach-koov] is sweet and savory, a bit tangy, with a nice soft texture to it. It is often paired with rich meats, as it cuts the potent flavor of it nicely.

Ingredients:

» 3 medium beets
» 1/4 of an onion
» 1 tsp of oil
» Juice of 1/2 of a large lemon
» Pinch of salt
» 1/2 tsp of sugar
» 1/2 tsp white vinegar

Instructions:

1 Preheat oven to 350°F/180°C. Cut stems off beets and scrub clean.

2 Bake covered for about 1 hour, or until soft. Take out and set aside to cool.

3 Once cooled off, peel and shred on the course side of a grater. Add chopped onion, oil, lemon juice, salt and sugar. Mix and refrigerate to cool.*

DESSERTS

CHEESECAKE
Sernik

PREP TIME: 20 MIN | COOK TIME: 1HR + COOLING

Sernik [sehr-neek] is a simple dessert, made from farmer's cheese and eggs with a few additions, but oh, so special and delicious. There are many varieties of it in Poland, this is the most simple and most traditional. Cheesecake, along with poppyseed roll, is a must-have Christmas dessert.

Ingredients:

» 2 lb / 1 kg of farmer's cheese
» 6 eggs, separated
» 1 cup / 110 g of powdered sugar
» 1 cup / 200 ml of heavy whipping cream
» 2 tbs of potato flour
» 1 tsp vanilla
» Pinch of salt
» 1 egg yolk
» 2 tbs of milk

Instructions:

1 Place farmer's cheese in a food processor with a blade attachment and blend until smooth (about 5-6 minutes) and until most lumps are gone.

2 Preheat oven to 330°F /165°C.

3 Separate egg yolks from egg whites and place egg yolks in a large mixing bowl. Add sugar and whisk on high for 2-3 minutes, until well blended.

4 In a separate bowl mix whipping cream with flour and vanilla.

5 Change whisk to a mixing paddle and add whipping cream mixture to egg/sugar mixture and mix just until combined. Continuously mixing add blended cheese. Mix just until blended.

6 In a separate bowl whisk egg whites with a pinch of salt to form a stiff foam. Gently fold into cheese mixture.

7 Prepare a 10 inch / 25 cm spring form by cutting out a circle in parchment paper big enough to cover the bottom. With a little bit of butter and your fingers grease the inner side of spring pan and sprinkle with bread crumbs. Shake off excess.

8 In a small bowl with a fork combine 1 egg yolk with milk.

9 Gently spoon cheese mixture into pan and even out. Spoon egg yolk/milk mixture onto the top on cheesecake batter.

10 Bake for 1 hour. If the top starts to brown too much, cover with a piece of tin foil. Turn oven off and let cake cool in the oven for about 10 minutes, then crack the door and let cool completely.

A note from <u>Anna</u>:

Best to let cheesecake rest in the fridge overnight before serving.

APPLE CAKE
Jabłecznik

PREP TIME: 45 MIN | COOK TIME: 45-50 MIN

Jabłecznik [yah-bweh-chnyik], a warm and tangy apple filling surrounded by a soft and flaky lemony crust, also known as szarlotka [shar-loh-tkah], is also one of my favorite cakes to be served around the holidays

Ingredients:

» CRUST:
» 2 1/2 cups of flour
» 1 whole egg
» 1 yolk (reserve the egg white)
» 1 cup of powdered sugar
» 14 tbs (2 sticks minus 2 tbs) / 200 g of butter
» 1 tsp of baking powder
» Zest of 1/2 lemon

» FILLING:
» 10 (about 1 lb) tart apples (I like Granny Smith)
» 1/4 cup of sugar
» Zest and juice of 1/2 lemon
» 1/4 tsp of cinnamon

Instructions:

1 To prepare the crust: whip the egg + egg yolk with sugar. Add flour, baking powder and lemon zest. Cut cold butter into smaller cubes and add to the mixture. Mix and knead until just combined with the help of a utensil. If you see lumps of butter in it, leave it. Butter will make the crust flaky.

2 Wrap in plastic wrap and refrigerate for at least 1 hour.

3 To make the filling: peel and core the apples. Shred on the course side of a grater, and add to a deep frying pan. Add sugar, zest and lemon juice and cook until all juice evaporates (about 30 minutes). Set aside to cool.

4 When ready to bake, preheat the oven to 400°F / 205°C.

5 Grease the bottom and sides of a 9 x 9 inch / 23 x 23 cm baking dish with butter or line with parchment paper.

6 Cut the dough in half and roll out (through parchment paper, to make it easier). Distribute evenly on the bottom and all the way up the sides. Scoop the cool filling onto the bottom of the curst. Roll out the remaining half of the dough and place on top of the filling.

7 Whisk the egg white with a teaspoon of water with a fork, and brush onto the top of the crust.

8 Bake for 45-50 minutes or until crust is golden brown.

A note from <u>Anna</u>:

* you can skip this step, and spread some marmalade on each slice before serving.

GINGER BREAD
Piernik

PREP TIME: 25 MIN | COOK TIME: 60 MIN

Piernik [pye-rnyeek] is a soft and aromatic cake. Flavors of cinnamon, ginger, allspice and cloves are primary, with hints of citrusy orange added to the mix. Dark chocolate glaze adds complexity and makes our taste buds even happier... who doesn't like chocolate?!

Ingredients:

» 2 tbs of honey
» 1 cup / 250 ml of milk
» 2 tbs of plum / strawberry / currant (or other favorite fruit) butter / marmalade
» Zest of 1/2 orange
» 1/2 tsp ground ginger
» 2 tsp of cinnamon
» 1/2 tsp of ground nutmeg
» 1/2 tsp of ground cloves
» 1/2 tsp of ground allspice
» 1/8 tsp of ground cardamom (optional)
» 9 tbs / 125 g of butter
» 2 eggs
» 1 cup / 250 g of granulated sugar
» 2 cups / 300 g of flour
» 1 tsp of baking soda
» 2 tsp of baking powder
» A pinch of salt

ADDITIONALLY:
» A few tablespoons of plum / strawberry / currant (or other favorite fruit) butter / marmalade

GLAZE:
» 1/2 cup of whipping cream
» 3.5 oz / 100 g of dark chocolate

Instructions:

1 In a small saucepan place honey, marmalade, orange zest and spices and heat through. Set aside to cool.

2 In a large mixing bowl beat butter and sugar. Add eggs one by one. Add honey mixture once it has cooled off. Stir well.

3 Preheat oven to 350°F / 180°C. Line a bread loaf pan with parchment paper.

4 Mix flour with baking powder, baking soda and salt. Add flour to sugar/butter mixture gradually and let combine well.

5 Transfer mixture into loaf pan and bake for 50-60 minutes, or until inserted toothpick comes out clean.

6 Cool bread completely before slicing in half horizontally from end to end. Spread marmalade onto the bottom part and return the top back onto the marmalade*.

7 To make the glaze, heat cream in a small saucepan. Remove from heat, add broken up chocolate. Mix until melted and smooth. Cool glaze slightly before pouring over ginger bread.

POPPY SEED ROLL
Makowiec

YIELDS: 2 – 13 INCH ROLLS | PREP TIME: 1.5 HRS | COOK TIME 45–50 MIN

Makowiec [mah-ko-vyets] is "officially" referred to as "strucla makowa". "Strucla" is a rolled yeast dough filled with a sweet filling of choice, poppy seed, sweet farmer's cheese, almonds, apples or jam.

Ingredients:

FILLING:
» About 17 oz / 500 g of raw black or blue poppy seeds*
» 3 cups / 750 ml of boiling water
» 4 oz / 100 g of butter
» 1 cup / 250 g of sugar
» 4 tbs of honey
» 3/4 cup / 100 g raisins
» 1 cup / 100 g walnuts

DOUGH:
» 3/4 cup / 150 ml of warm milk
» 1/2 cup / 110 g of sugar
» 1 1/2 tbs of dry active yeast
» 3 1/2 cups / 500 g of all purpose flour
» 1 egg plus 2 yolks (large eggs)
» 2 oz / 50 g of butter
» Pinch of salt

GLAZE:
» 5 tbs / 55 g of powdered sugar
» 2 tbs of lemon juice
» 1 tbs of hot water
» 3-5 tbs of orange peel or sliced almonds

Instructions:

1 Place raisins in hot water (or rum, whiskey or brandy) and set aside to soak.

2 Warm milk slightly, add yeast and sugar and set aside in a warm spot for 10 minutes. Melt butter and set aside to cool slightly.

3 To make dough, place flour in a mixing bowl. Whisk egg with egg yolks and add to flour. Add milk/sugar/yeast mixture and start combining. Add melted butter and work to combine all ingredients. Add a few tablespoons of milk if dough is too dry. Dough should have consistency of play-dough – not sticky but pliable. Once a dough ball is formed, cover and set aside in a warm place for at least 1 hour.

4 To make filling, place poppy seeds in a pot, add boiling water and soak for 10 minutes, then boil for 20-25 minutes. Add a bit more water if they get dry, enough to cover. Drain well. Once it cools slightly you will have to put it through a meat grinder with the fine grinding plate – TWICE.

5 In a large skillet or a pot heat butter, add poppy seeds, sugar, honey, drained raisins and mix well. Heat through and mix until sugar is dissolved. Add crushed walnuts and mix. Set aside to cool. Whip egg whites with a pinch of salt until stiff. Add to poppy seed mixture and fold in gently.

6 Once the dough rises, divide in half. Roll out each half into a rectangular shape (30 x 25 cm / 12 x 9 inch). Place rolled out dough onto parchment paper large enough to go around your roll twice. Place half of the filling on the first rectangle leaving a bit of space on each side(** see photos). Roll starting from the shorter side, pinch the ends together as you go along. Wet the edge with water or egg white for better seal.

7 Once rolled, make sure to leave on parchment paper with the long seam down. Roll parchment paper around the poppy seed roll twice, leaving space for roll to "grow" (about 3/4 inch / 2 cm). Make sure the end of the paper is under the roll. Set aside in a warm place to rise for about 30-45 minutes.

8 Do the same with the second roll.

9 When ready to bake, heat oven to 350°F / 180°C. Place in hot oven and bake for 40-50 minutes. Remove and cool.

10 To make glaze, mix powdered sugar with lemon juice. Add hot water teaspoon at a time and whisk to combine. It should make a thick paste. If it comes out too watery, add more powdered sugar. Spoon onto each roll. Sprinkle with orange peel or almond shavings. Let set.

11 Slice at an angle to serve.

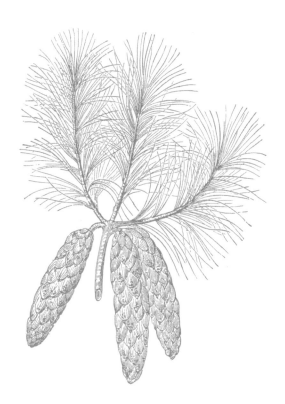

You can prepare this dessert a couple of days before the big day. It will do well stored in the fridge or a cold basement.

A note from <u>Anna</u>:

Cookies can be made several days before Christmas and stored in a dry spot in the kitchen. The challenge will then be keeping away from them, but that's a whole other story.

SHORTBREAD COOKIES
Ciastka Kruche

PREP TIME: 10 MIN | COOK TIME: 8-12 MIN EACH

In Polish, they are called ciastka kruche [chia-stkah kroo-heh], meaning crumbly cookies, because of their delicate, buttery and flaky nature. They are not super sweet, so please keep an open mind, but that just means you can eat a lot more.

Ingredients:

» 2 cups of all purpose flour
» 3 egg yolks (reserve whites)
» 10 tbs / 140 g of butter
» 1/2 cup of powdered sugar
» 1/2 tsp of vanilla extract
» 1/4 cup of sour cream
» 2 tsp of baking powder
» Pinch of salt

Instructions:

1 Place flour in a mixing bowl, add butter cut into small pieces, and the rest of the ingredients. Gently mix with hands until just combined and form a dough ball. Don't work it too much, as it will make for a dense cookie.

2 When combined and you still see bits of butter, it's okay. Butter will melt while baking and make for a flaky cookie. Wrap the dough ball in plastic and refrigerate for an hour.

3 When ready, preheat oven to 350°F / 180°C, divide the ball into smaller portions and roll out onto a floured surface to about a 3/8 - 1/4 inch / 0.5 cm thickness. Using your favorite cookie cutter cut out shapes and place onto a baking sheet covered with parchment paper.

4 Slightly beat egg whites with a fork and using a kitchen brush, brush each cookie with egg whites and sprinkle with a pinch of sugar.

5 Bake for about 10-12 minutes, or until golden brown.

CHRISTMAS FRUIT CAKE *Keks*

YIELDS: 1 LOAF PAN | PREP TIME: 15 MIN | COOK TIME: 45-50 MIN

This is not your average fruitcake. Keks świąteczny [kehx sh-viow-teh-chnyh] is not dry and heavy, but instead soft, lightly sweet and studded with a balanced variety of dried fruit and nuts. It will completely bust the bad rep of mass-made fruitcake.

Ingredients:

- » 1 lb / 500 g of mixed dried fruit and nuts - raisins, mangos, prunes, walnuts, almonds
- » 2 sticks / 225 g of butter at room temperature
- » 1 cup of powdered sugar
- » 5 eggs - whites and yolks separated
- » 1 tbs of baking powder
- » 2 cups of all purpose flour
- » 1 tsp of vanilla extract
- » Pinch of salt

Instructions:

1 Preheat oven to 350°F / 180°C.

2 Crush and slice dried fruit and nuts.

3 Cream butter with sugar until well combined and fluffy. Add egg yolks one by one and keep mixing. Add vanilla extract and gradually add flour mixed with baking powder. Finally add fruit/nut mixture.

4 Whisk egg whites with salt on high until stiff foam forms. Gently fold into fruit-cake batter until well combined.

5 Transfer batter into a loaf pan lined with parchment paper and bake at 350°F / 180°C for 20 minutes. Turn heat down to 325°F / 160°C and bake for another 30-40 minutes, until a toothpick inserted into cake comes out clean and top of the cake is golden brown. If top is browning too fast, cover with aluminum foil.

6 With the help of a small strainer sprinkle with powdered sugar before serving.

THANKS

Special thanks to my husband Mark, for motivating me to push on, always having my back, being my biggest fan, best tester, taster and food critique. Thank you for your honesty and unconditional love.

Thank you to my parents for opening the world to me and allowing me to be my own person.

Dziękuję moim rodzicom za otwarcie mi ścieżki na świat i pozwolenie na bycie sobą.

Thanks to Wendy Taylor and Joshua Wilson for providing me with superb proofreading and editing skills, and to Igor Wypijewski for exceptional graphic design advice.

I couldn't have done it without your support, and for that I am exceptionally grateful.

IMPORTANT NOTES

Safe Minimum Internal Temperature Chart

Follow safe food handling rules, as recommended by the USDA (United States Department of Agriculture).

Safe steps in food handling, cooking, and storage are essential in preventing foodborne illness. You can't see, smell, or taste harmful bacteria that may cause illness. In every step of food preparation, follow the four guidelines to keep food safe:

Clean — Wash hands and surfaces often.

Separate — Separate raw meat from other foods.

Cook — Cook to the right temperature.

Chill — Refrigerate food promptly.

Cook all food to these minimum internal temperatures as measured with a food thermometer before removing food from the heat source. For reasons of personal preference, consumers may choose to cook food to higher temperatures.

Product	Minimum Internal Temperature & Rest Time
Beef, Pork, Veal & Lamb Steaks, chops, roasts	145 °F (62.8 °C) and allow to rest for at least 3 minutes
Ground meats	160 °F (71.1 °C)
Ham, fresh or smoked (uncooked)	145 °F (62.8 °C) and allow to rest for at least 3 minutes
Fully Cooked Ham	(to reheat) Reheat cooked hams packaged in USDA-inspected plants to 140 °F (60 °C) and all others to 165 °F (73.9 °C)

Product	Minimum Internal Temperature
All Poultry (breasts, whole bird, legs, thighs, wings, ground poultry, giblets, and stuffing)	165 °F (73.9 °C)
Eggs	160 °F (71.1 °C)
Fish & Shellfish	145 °F (62.8 °C)
Leftovers	165 °F (73.9 °C)
Casseroles	165 °F (73.9 °C)

Source: this page: https://www.fsis.usda.gov/safetempchart

Wild Mushrooms

Only consume wild mushrooms obtained from known sources. Do not assume all mushrooms are edible. It is not safe to serve wild mushrooms to children. Please do your research before allowing children to consume dishes containing wild mushrooms.

Food is the flavor of life

Made in United States
Orlando, FL
24 October 2022